# EVERYTHING ALIVE

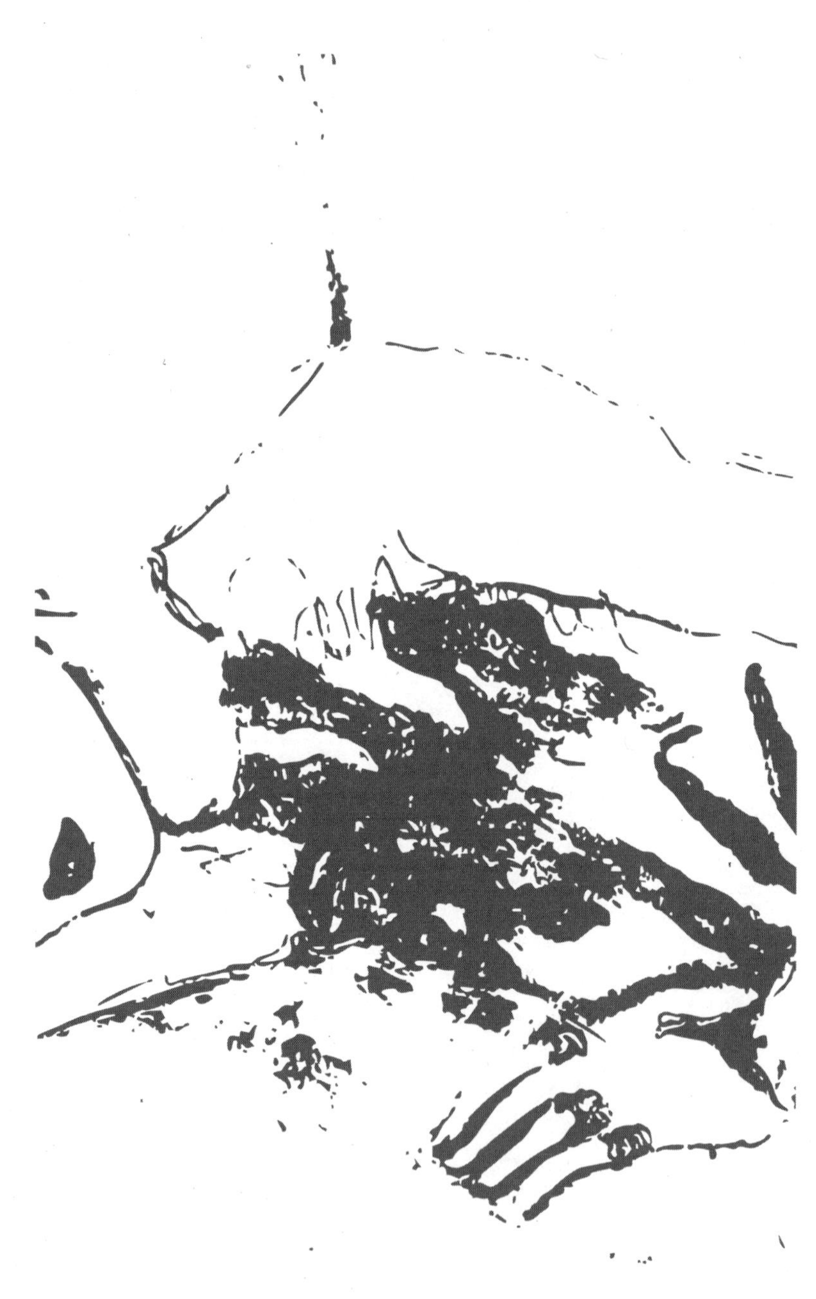

# EVERYTHING ALIVE

POEMS

Molly Johnsen

GREEN WRITERS PRESS *Brattleboro, Vermont*

Copyright © 2025 Molly Johnsen

All rights reserved. No part of this book may be reproduced in any form or by any means, electronic or mechanical, including photocopying, recording, or by any information storage and retrieval system, without permission in writing from the publisher.

Please note that no part of this book may be used or reproduced in any manner for the purpose of training artificial intelligence technologies or systems. No AI was used in the material herein.

Printed in the United States

10 9 8 7 6 5 4 3 2 1

Green Writers Press is a Vermont-based publisher whose mission is to spread a message of hope and renewal through the words and images we publish. Throughout we will adhere to our commitment to preserving and protecting the natural resources of the earth. To that end, a percentage of our proceeds will be donated to environmental activist groups. Green Writers Press gratefully acknowledges support from individual donors, friends, and readers to help support the environment and our publishing initiative.

Green Writers press

*Giving Voice to Writers & Artists Who Will Make the World a Better Place*
Green Writers Press | Brattleboro, Vermont
www.greenwriterspress.com

ISBN: 979-8-9914134-6-6

COVER ART BY LEIGH VINER

PRINTED ON 100% PCW RECYCLED PAPER BY BOOKMOBILE.
BASED IN MINNEAPOLIS, MINNESOTA, BOOKMOBILE BEGAN AS A DESIGN AND TYPESETTING PRODUCTION HOUSE IN 1982, AND STARTED OFFERING PRINT SERVICES IN 1996.
BOOKMOBILE IS RUN ON 100% WIND- AND SOLAR-POWERED CLEAN ENERGY.

*For my family.*

*For Lee.*

# Contents

*I.*

## II.



## III.



## IV.

V.

# I.

## After the Accident

I wake
in the hospital bed, my body
torn, my clothing
removed, but I know to reach
for my mother as if
she's just been born
from my womb:
mother to daughter to
mother—our naked same hands
touching her head on my chest
as I bleed in the aftermath
of a beginning.

# My Body is Full of Things That Aren't Mine

When I opened my eyes, I knew hands had been inside me. Between my legs up into my pelvis and under my ribs. Bones split like shards of black sky in lightning. My ribcage was re-secured around my still-beating heart. My skin was stitched. They left metal there. They left the room after promising my body it could still grow around a baby if I wanted it to. I imagined you.

## A Year and a Half

*Put your heads down on your desks,*
Mrs. C used to say,
*and sit up when you think a minute has passed.*

I'd count to sixty and resurface,
always first. The second hand ticking
through what was left to endure.

When I told Dad about my trouble,
he tugged on my earlobes:
*Your brain runs fast. You get that from me.*

Dad's watch is always set twenty minutes ahead.

Recently, he told me the tumor had metastasized.
Afterward, I chose a wedding date—

*Don't pick your head up for a year and a half.*

At some point, time stopped feeling
like something to sit through. Now,
I check to see how much is gone.

It was always so lonely, raising my head
to a room of bent-in-half bodies.
Why didn't I bury my face back into my palms?

Dad likes to look at his watch and know
what he sees won't be true till the future.

The numbers say he's late
but don't worry, he tells me,
*I'll be there.*

## Undone

*1991*

I was three, and you hid
*The Little Princess* from me
because I ran to you sobbing
when Richard Greene repeated a
hollow, aching call for his daughter.
"Saa-raah," a slow pendulum swing.
Body contained by plaster, he was
wheelchair-bound in a world of
black and white.
His blind eyes made me cry;
Sarah stood facing him, and
he couldn't find her.

*2015*

The surgeries were mostly over,
but a tube still pushed itself down my throat.

Then you were there, said my name;
          I recalled the firetruck,
          scissors cutting
          shirt from body.
I tried and failed to speak.

Yellow liquid in the bag beside me.
Cellophaned sandwich on a pink plastic tray.
Your hands were cold.

Machines beeped, and I willed myself back to bed
While my lacerated liver regenerated.

*1991*

Thoughts of the bandaged man
stayed with me for months.
The VHS tape was taking cover somewhere.
At random, that blank, blind face sprang,
snake-in-a-can, out of my brain.

One night, alone in the kitchen,
I dragged a chair to the fridge,
climbed on top, and
tiptoed to my peak.
I pushed the Cheerios aside,
wobbled, stretched, caught my breath:
felt around,
found it.

## Buffalo Nickel

*For my grandmother*

I keep your rosary beads in my desk drawer—
I hold them when I ask you for things.

I'm sorry I treat whatever's up there like it only exists
to give me what I need—

not to guide or advise me, but make my wedding day
sunny. Your belief sent you where I won't end up.

My night sky, when the clouds allow, is all stars and moon.
My body—blood and water, mostly—

will end as dirt or ash. My heart is a muscle, my love
stops in my skull. No, in my brain, which I'm told is messed up.

If someone or something up in the skyceiling made me
this way, then I have a longer list of enemies.

I'm not saying it's impossible to hum one's soul
into another realm, to chant from the deepbelly and end up

elsewhere, to look at the sky and see unnamable beauty
aglow. Sounds nice. But I'm too full of the stuff

you'd have me purged of. Hate, for one. My body holds it.
I hate this messed-up body. And my own mother

sometimes. But I keep a glass dish on my desk,
filled with coins dulled by time. Heads-up pennies

and that Buffalo nickel a neighbor gave to me.
*For luck,* he explained. *Can't hurt.*

## When Asked If I Saw the White Light

Pain blazed in my eyes under the light
they angled to see me by.

The Nation's-Best weren't sure they could tidy
the mess of me. No monitor predicted *Yes*.

Here's what I saw: the glow
of open ambulance doors,

the black backs of my eyelids,
my neon sneaker in the street.

We bleed.
We're manhandled

by mortality. No brightness
undarkens what dying looks like.

# Mondays at Four

The therapist hands me two pieces of plastic—
black, white. One for each palm. A wire transmits
a loop of pulses from her controls to my fists.
Black, white; back, forth, my mind gymnastics
back to the accident. My spool of memory loosens.

*Tell me when you feel safe.* I wait awhile, tell her.
(It's a lie.) The scene I create is spare as a child's painting—
two jointless bodies, stick-limbed. Open space between
land and sky. My black, unceasing blood is a river
on the bridge above the river. Emma's face
in the headlights, shaped like screaming.

## Follow-Up with the Orthopedist

On the exam table, what I feel isn't pain—it's a man too close to my face. I want my home to have a moat. I want to swim around the yard in circles, watch the light yellow the windows, feel elbows and knees push water away. Or,

I want my mouth to be a moat. I want my eyes to be windows. I'll raise the shades when I decide it's time. In my bodyhouse, ottomans sit like guard dogs beside the armchairs. A pot of cooling soup on the counter holds enough for one. This man can't enter unless I lower the creaking bridge. I'll do it slowly. Then I'll be the one who gives instructions. Shoes come off at the door. He will compliment me on my ottomans. He can't bust in to my limbs and move them in circles, can't force my body back flat. I won't talk about pain. Won't let him near my face.

## what we share

or what if trauma is like sourdough
starter? We all have a mother. Wild

yeast can be finicky as memory,
adapting to the climate it finds

itself in: San Francisco, Denver,
Connecticut, me. Passed around

between bodies, not mason jars,
but—like a good loaf—we're hardened

and split. Feed a starter regularly
with flour and water and it remains

active. We eat each other's
beginnings. Your self-dealing dad

becomes my seizure in the street, your
drug addiction my fear of black

cars. Half the blood in my body
comes from other people. My cousin

tried to smuggle his starter into Spain—
only wanted to eat his own in his bread.

## Alone Together

The wind shakes
the moon till it blinks
behind leaves like
headlights:
you say, breathe.

I'm only a piece of the me
you never got to see.
Or maybe it's the other
way around: maybe I'm
more of me now. Bones
strengthen after breaking.

Toes on cold tile, we
see each other
side-by-side, we
watch each other
brush our teeth.
I spit white foam, afraid
you know—
I'm an emergency.

# Sex Now

The woman in white lubes her gloved fingers, enters
me and pokes around. She notes my U-shaped scar tissue
and sends me home with a dildo because I need to
loosen up. She tells me to imagine that my vagina is a
clock: pushing straight down is six, up by my
clit: high noon. *Have your partner press each*
*number.* I always wince at one and nine.

I ache to come home from work someday, kick
off my shoes and mount you. I want to push you against
a windowpane in the middle of *The Sopranos*, or take you
while you're showering—bite your neck and chin.
We can't fuck until I'm wet and wide: *think of*
*how balloons expand*. But to me that means a clown
twisting dogs from cock-shaped tubes.

Lube, dildo, balloon, breathe;
now we check the clock.

When you're inside of me, I remember
metal there. Blood on black, burst
bladder, "vaginal packing." I try to feel
you as you are, but there are spots of
numbness, and, no, don't move like that.

One day we'll fuck in a field of corn or an
alleyway at night. For now I ignore the clown
and feel your weight on mine. Your skin's softer
than metal, and I forget how to tell time.

## Dust

Here I am,
unpacking half a home.

Your dust has traveled in the wax
of my candles, the pages of my books.

if you shed yourself
into candle wax,

are you ever coming
back? Our key doesn't fit

in my new door, which swells
in this humidity and drags

against the slanted boards.
Getting home means adding

half-moon scratches to the floor
like proof that I exist.

I'll come and go,
shake snow off boots, carry

mail and bags of food. I'll lose
my skin to self-made grooves.

## Your First Visit to Syracuse

When I told you the brand-new-
penny sun over the lake looked
like a harvest moon, you said
*But it's the sun*, which I knew.
We drove on, a shifting
sense of *should we stop*
*to see the view?*
Instead, we went back and mounted
an art deco mirror on my new wall.
In it, we watched your fractured
body move. All weekend,
you were someone
else. You were
The One Who
Will Fly to JFK on Sunday.
Your smile took
longer. I noticed myself notice
the red in your beard here.
When I cried in the parking lot
of Liquor City, you took me
in your arms and carried
me to my car. Now,
you're in Brooklyn, on a couch—
the one I didn't take—
and it's Sunday, so you're
eating Chinese food. I walk
to Walgreens and buy a frozen
burrito and some beer. No moon tonight.
Or maybe I can't see it from here.

# In Italy, On a Boat, In a Cave, On a Boat, In Italy

God carved the Virgin from this
stone, apparently. My heart was
made in the dark of my mother; her
body surrounded the start of my own
—the way the earth holds the
horizon. Birth is the beginning of an
echo. In this divinity of dark, God's
daughter won't take shape for me—
like the woman trapped in my own
body cage. I yearn to give birth to
her. Anchored here, we bend our
knees to stay steady. We point up at
rock—at where the sky should be—
while our boat rocks in the wake
of another.

# Like Apple from Seed

When nights were still scary, our father used to
tell us about the moon: hooked and hanging
on a bamboo fishing pole. Held by a man drifting

in a spaceboat, he reeled it in only in daylight.
When story time became my job, I told you the moonman
was slowly consuming his catch: mouth full of cool white

on those nights made only of black, so the moon
came back new and grew like apple from seed,
like me and you and the tree where we now stand.

You're a head and neck taller than me, and you say
*It's beautiful.* But I see that the moon will weigh down
the branch till it cracks then rots away—
or maybe I can climb up

toward where it's stuck. The rain starts, and we're here
getting sucked up and swallowed. *I have to save it,* I say.
And you make of your hands a stirrup.

# II.

# Epilepsy,

The first time you shook me, I was small enough to
fit into my father's arms. He was carrying me to the
car—sunlight made winter glare whiter around us.
You took hold of me from somewhere under my skin,
pulling my eyes back into my head. Dad knelt down in
the snow. My shivers weren't from the cold. *Molly*, he
said. *Molly*. I was too young to know my own name.
I imagine him in the red coat I've seen in old photos:
too big for him. There, in the driveway of 90 Arnold
Avenue. He cradled my body, brought it into the
kitchen's indifferent hum, and cried while he waited
for you to leave me.

*Spontaneous spirit possession.*

You returned a year later, but still before memory took
root in me. Again, winter and my father. He strung
together a theory for the doctors, something about
the way the sun came through the trees as we drove:
bright, then gone. Bright, then gone. They told him
you would forget me. *Febrile*, they said.
*It's common*. He hung a T-shirt in the window
next to my car seat.

*Punishment for a broken taboo.*

Two decades later, you came back. They say it's
because I bled out between a truck and a guardrail.

I didn't hit my head, but you found my broken body anyway. Maybe you'd been lying in wait all along.

*An affliction of persons who have sinned against the moon.*

The first time you got me after that, I was reading the newspaper aloud to Alex. You took hold for only a moment, allowing me to stay conscious. Later, I'd learn to call this "partial." I didn't have your full attention. Or you didn't need mine.

*The Falling Sickness.*

You made the living room unfamiliar. I fell onto the couch as you pushed an animal howl from my mouth. When you left, my dad's fingers were bleeding. He'd tried to hold my tongue down. You allow me the memory of my father's hands, his face in that room: he was seeing me for the first time, trying to decide whether to run away or freeze in place.

*Satanic Interference.*

So many words have taken on weight since you came back: generalize, tonic, cluster, aura.

*Mad Pig Disease.*

You start slow, growing from the back of my brain. You dizzy me. I feel stoned on deja vu. *It's like a sixth sense*, I've said. All I mean is you're impossible to describe. That's another way you taunt me, another way you take language away.

*Punishment for a pregnant adulteress.*

And who am I without language?
Skin, skeleton, and you.

*Black Magic.*

Once, you got me in the middle of the street, pulled the crosswalk out from under me. When the world reappeared, I watched my apples roll away. *Those are apples. They're rolling.* Strangers bent over me: *Are you okay?* You grasped my poison brain like a knuckly witch. I didn't know how to say *I'm okay.*

*The Shaking Syndrome.*

When Becca saw you come upon me, she filmed it for the doctor. I'd prepared her for you: *If it happens, you have to. They need to see.* In the video, I'm told, you open my mouth, make it cry out. They say the shot is unsteady, and Becca's saying *Molly* behind the screen. As you left, you handed me jealousy—of Becca, for what she'd been allowed to see. You leave me out. I only have what I'm told and what you cackle before blacking me out. I'll never watch the video, though. You come, but you always go. The video would stay with me.

*The Holy Illness.*

We try to see you on monitor screens. Doctors in white coats track your progress. Their explanations are flimsy, thin with sighs. *We can't know.* They wire me up and send me into the sun with a head wrapped in white gauze, like a wounded soldier in a low-budget movie. You rarely show up when I'm wearing those wires. You know better than to visit when you might be seen. It's only then that I try to summon you, ache to find a trace. But you and I are well-acquainted now, and I can feel your absence behind my eyes.

*The Disease of the People with Burns.*

Last time you arrived, pulled my brain into my throat, you stayed partial and I wrote. I'd been at my computer, so I decided to see what would come out if I turned you into the words you allowed my brain to save. *Here I got,* I wrote, *writing during the XOXO carp fart damn kiss 90 avenue armond arnold finally i got it.*

*Rapture.*

# III.

# Flight

A leaf turns
into a hand—
veined and open.
The yolk
of an egg cracked
into a bowl
is the sun
of last summer in France
where we ate sour grapes
from the vine.
A can of ginger beer rolls
around in the fridge:
the last one
he ever bought.
Stars are gods
or eyes. Nighttime
decides. I unfold
an origami crane, lay it flat
and it's my skin: scarred
by someone's careful work.
Holding the paper square, I turn
myself into a bird.
Up here, the clouds billow over
my unscarred body.

# Inside / Out

The pits of cherries aren't fruit, but seed. Buried
inside their orbs, they exist to make
more. The pits contain cyanide and can kill
us if we try hard enough—if we eat them one
after another after another. I'm used to having pieces

of foreign things inside me; I couldn't
tell you how much metal is holding
my body together. They say I can have a baby.
Will I feel like my child is part of me

completely, or will I simply be growing something
to release to the outside? The day we ate
cherries on the beach we decided they're
a worse version of grapes. Spat pits into sand.

What do we do when we find ourselves
outside of ourselves? When asked for the story,
I watch myself tell it. I've begun to wonder
if it actually happened to me.

They say you don't want to lose the pain
of loss because it's all you have left
of the thing. I can run loops around the park—
miles and miles without stopping.

## After the Grocery Store

I seize in the middle of the street
after my aura drowns me in                    spotlight.

It creeps up from the back
corners of my brain like deja vu.
I'll show you

what I see. No, what I visualize:
a big-toothed mouth, then a hand pushes out from inside.

The hand reaches, and I lose speech to the brain-seen
teeth. I am consumed, and I seize.          Call me a witch
or a mystic.

I am carrying groceries.          Are you with me?
When I wake, I see gaping mouths of passersby
who've watched  my convulsing body contort itself

in the crosswalk. My need now is sleep. My brain
is rigged. I find one                    word in my mouth: *Friends*.
I say it again and again

like I'm proud of it. Watch my chicken salad roll
away. *Where. Friends*. A woman nearby gives me

sorry eyes. My apartment is pointing
distance away. *Honey*, she crouches down, *you were*
*alone.*                    Still with me now?  Who is she

to know. I won't be able to use my keys.
*Need*. I hear sirens; no one explains                    why.

## Self Portrait as a Chair

In ninth grade, Mrs. G asked us to make negative space
from construction paper and white cardstock.

She put a kitchen chair on a table and told us
to cut black shapes and mark where the chair wasn't.

Everyone got to cutting and gluing.
Chair after chair appeared, defined

by black bits of nothing on a blank white field.
Mine looked like a kindergartner's paper snowflake.

I got a C. It was the worst grade I ever got in anything.
So now, when they run hours-long memory tests on me

at the neurologist, I refuse certain parts.
The one where they hold up a geometric sketch,

flip it over and say, *Draw it.*
The one where I make triangles

into a perfect square. Instead,
I sit back, cross my arms, and say no.

Epilepsy made me into
a mind trick. We still wait the full minute.

It feels good to fail willingly, to show off
what my brain can't do.

Part of me will be marked down
in a column called "Worrisome,"

but I can say *Told you so.*

## Good Morning

*It's psychotic* she says *that you count out the almonds before you put them in the blender.* She smiles into her coffee. Here's something I've never told her: years ago, after the stoned teenage driver put me in the ICU, I used to ask the nurses to draw a chart on the whiteboard in my room listing what medications I'd take that day, how many and how soon. I couldn't see the sun, so I learned to tell the time by what had a line through it: two rounds of oxy and a valium meant early afternoon. Fourteen almonds is what the recipe calls for. I sip my insane smoothie and run through a mental inventory of the fridge. We have spinach. Later, I go to the store for chicken. In the hospital, every night, the same nurse handed me the same menu. I'd check off "yogurt parfait," and it would arrive the next morning at six on a tray.

## A Letter to My Brain

I want you back. These days, you're only whole
on monitor screens—circuit-mazed, your nooks
rendered neon in patterns I wait for others
to discern. Seizure-made scars like scorched
earth. You scare me. You're like a stranger

on the street yelling my name.
When did I start fearing
you? The world shouldn't
blur into waves, but you taunt me that way.

I walk and I pray you'll let me live
out the hour without echoes of half-true
deja vu. Doctors glue braids of wire to my scalp.
I'm a coop most of you has flown.

All I ask is for some sort of steady.
Instead, you short out, and I drop
a mug of tea on my shoes. I want to re-seed
myself, to see the past without squinting.

I want my patchy vocabulary to burst
at the seams. You are holes and heaps
of cold air—winter coming through
cracks. When will the shriek of sun on snow

feel safe again? When will alone feel like home
rather than a storm I have to prepare for? The pills
you make me take slow me down, and I wake
with dried spit on my face. Have mercy.
At your worst, you allow me the sun-warmed mud
of true love, but not to recall how I felt when I found it.

## Mother/Daughter

We take the subway to dinner. We're underwater most of the way.
Later, you get so drunk you can't chew your food.
Then you tell me you're afraid I won't be able to have a baby.

In my favorite home movie, you're giving me a bath. *Whose arm is this?* you ask.
*Whose leg? Whose nose?* You trace the outline of the birthmark on my thigh, tilt
my head back to rinse out the shampoo. I close my eyes when you tell me to.

*I'll have a baby,* I say to you, and the room, and the tug at my chest.

A month ago, you hugged my body while it convulsed on the couch.
When I came to, I thought your screams came from my mouth.

## For My Father

Aunt Amy's funeral was yesterday,
and you stayed seated except

to give a toast. Later, you told me
the ache in your back kept you

in your chair. The doctors say
it's in your bones.

Last time we visited,
you helped Amy use a straw

and sang her show tunes we all
swore she recognized. Her illness

always felt like the only thing in the room.
Yours can hide in a folding chair.

If I'd known how you hurt
when you stand, I would've told you

to sit and lowered the rest
of the earth to the floor.

# Photos from Before the Divorce

I am holding a thin ribbon attached to a translucent balloon.
My father holds me in the sun-filtered bedroom.

Here I push my brother on the swing,
tiptoeing to reach his yellow plastic seat.

My fingers are tiny.
White cotton dress smudged with mud.

My dad hung that swing
on our maple tree.

We used to tap it for sap in the winter.
My mom, bent in the raspberry patch, next to the peach tree.

The only peaches I remember
were either too green or rotting.

A gallon of sap made a teaspoon of sweet.
My mother holds me on her hip.

Her pregnant stomach grapefruit-veined,
my father's arms, sunned and young;

I remember the banister where they rested
the camera and set the self-timer for this one–

they're naked. We all are. Funny in our purity:

the happiness, the skin, the camera's
almost-right position. Sure, I know now

what might repel me, but look—
stripped bare, we're all happy.

# All Sunlight

At dinner tonight, Sam's kids
are bright and round. The girl's too small
to speak, the boy has a lot of opinions.

Sam asks if I ever shared a bedroom
with my brother. I tell a truth:
*no, but we lived in an old, falling-down house.*

I never want anyone to believe I have more
than my share—of money, or pride.
Vacation time. Pie. The boy looks up at me:

wide, unyielding eyes.
*Why did you live in a falling down house?*
I clarify. *You're right,* my hand

reaching to the curve
of his shoulder, *It was just old.*

The boy moves away, satisfied. I want
a baby. A house for the baby, all sunlight
all the time. Sam's chickens squawk.

They lay the best eggs in Vermont. I don't need
more eggs. I need less of this sense that it's all
falling down all the time.

How do I learn to accept
the eggs I'll be offered? To choose
one type of truth and stick to it?
The boy turns toward his ice cream.
*I helped paint it,* I say. *It was full of big rooms.*

## Miracle

Our summer feet swung
over the Seine. Your
eyes were wet. The sun
soaked us both. The ice
cream in my cone dripped
onto my wrist. No ring, no
bent knee, no aisle. Just an
island, a river, a breeze, you
shaping the wave of me.

## Socks at the Beach

I used to wear socks to the beach
so my ankle wounds could keep to themselves,
no sun to darken the scars they were trying
to turn into. Now, I wear my scars like socks,

ones I picked out for myself. If I got to decide
what my new skin looked like, I'd turn my ankles into
the story I don't know how to stop telling. I'd keep
my mouth closed while everyone ran over my

hurt with their hands. No one knows about
the four perfect incisions on my abdomen,
scarred over now, but permanent signs
of others' intrusion. I only look at that section

of myself by accident. If I got to decide what my body
looked like, I'd be a straight line. Invisible
if I turned to the side. No pelvis for strangers' hands
to fix. No skin to de-elasticize. The meds kicked in

before I could give permission, so instead
I said *thank you.* And I never got to ask
what I look like inside. Now, I ask
my splotchy ankles to announce themselves,
uncovered. Signs of my healing:
imperfect but all on my own.

# IV.

## The Cu-Chi Tunnels, Vietnam

*For Natasha*

We descend; earth closes
in—its breath dampening
our skin. Echoes of decades-old
moans, gained ground, Viet Cong solders'
open, breathless mouths. They had no sense
of the end I move toward now. You trace

your fingertips over the walls
as if it's all the sleeping face
of a lover. I burrow bent-limbed
to black in the hand-made hollows
of someone else's land. They warned us
we could leave. I've never held myself

well in spaces that hold
me. Later,
you'll say you found
yourself on this war-torn ground.
You want to run

your tongue up and down
this country; I want to find light
and get out. Lungs wrung
tight like those smoke-filled nights
in your station wagon, driving
the curves of the beach without

headlights. Windows closed, ocean-coated
towels heaped in the back seat,
and the moon, always. We knew
nothing about what to look
out for. Sometimes

I worry that I exist
only where others can see. Here,
underground, you find
my hand and help it
to a ladder. But now I go up
and you stay down.

## Devil's Ivy

Pothos vines murder some of their own limbs
so others stay alive. The plant on our shelf
sends bone-dry leaves to the floor. A man
in grey scrubs once told me that my womb
is one of a woman who's given birth
three times. *Lucky her,* I thought.

When I read that pothos plants can bloom,
I assumed our mass of bloodthirsty branches
meant I'd failed at nurturing. I sometimes feel
nothing when you're inside me. It's not you—
it's just hard to figure out what's dead and why.

# We All Just Want to Make More of Ourselves

I can't call it a family home—the words don't ring
true. It's more like a pinecone. Resin-stained

seeds are my parents, brother and me. We wait
in our woody rooms for the season to turn—

we'll all plant ourselves elsewhere.
          What became of that house?

Pinecones can be placed under pillows
to conjure fertility. I was born

from unripe fruits. A seed
made from seeds.

Emptied cones fall and decompose.
Now here I am, in my home,

hoping that stand-alone tub
still exists: claw feet digging into tile floor.

## Some of the Things I Didn't Say in Albany

I miss my hospital bed. I miss having my pulse
checked four times a day. Doctors complimenting
my X-rays. Apple juice.

When we walk into your dad's room, he's retching
into a pink plastic tub. I hold you.

You spoon-feed your dad Jell-O. I wonder whether
I'll ever feed anything to you in a hospital bed.

Before we leave, we tuck him in and kiss his head.
Machines beep, morphine drips him to sleep. I remember
morphine: it's like being sung to.

Fresh air undoes nothing. I say I'm hungry, but I just want
to name my own need.

When we try to sleep, the bed feels too big.
Like it's meant for more than our bodies.

## Love, Me

Please, Love, breathe
into the back of my neck.

Curve a C around me.
Come here. Like this.

Make of us a nest, Love.
Show me my body's not

empty.

## Red Spots

Way back, when red spots meant chicken pox,
I wanted them so badly. Wanted cookies and the couch
and someone to care for me, and then to get better
and tell the whole playground about it. Last night,

you watched me measure the width
of our living room on my knees with a ruler
so I could buy a rug online. *I need to feel settled,* I said,
then I made you promise not to stain the rug
that doesn't exist. Later, you had to rub my back
to get me to breathe. I'm afraid to become a wreck

at the bottom of a lake—or a ceaseless storm, or a doll
who's really sick. When my doll came down with
magic marker blotches, Mom said dolls can't be cured.
She said they stay that way.

# You Taught Me Fear

You warned me about umbrellas.
I'd face years of bad luck if I opened one
inside. Same thing if I broke a mirror.
I remember humming till the end of tunnels,
tiptoeing over cracks in concrete.

We walked downstairs backwards
on the first of the year. I learned
to ward off the bad by considering
the worst outcome all the time. But when
a truck's bumper split my liver in half,
the organ healed on its own.

At the start of that day, I was headed to a house
on a pond in Rhode Island. No misstep
led me to the car fire on a bridge. I haven't told
you that the mirror in my apartment is cracked.
In it, I'm broken. Out here, I'm whole.

## Glitch

Dad taped over the part where Bambi's mom
gets shot. He did it one night while we were asleep—
didn't want us to know about Bad Guys.

I used to wonder why the Celtics always played
for a moment in the middle of the movie,
but I never thought to ask why Bambi's mom
made herself scarce after the glitch.

I was in second grade when Alexandra died.
She and I had eaten chocolate cupcakes high up
in the treehouse the week before. I didn't cry.
*Bambi* didn't teach me how much luck
it takes to stay alive.

And now I'm thirty-two,
and Dad's dying and I can't figure out why.
I don't know enough about blood cell counts,
can't grasp the word *metastasize.*
Someone pressed play but no one
taught me how to find the game.

# I Take the Kayak Out Alone

Two loons, side by side, they either know the answer
to everything or don't feel a need to. No other way

to stay at rest like that. The sun smoothes the lake,
the loons are used to this. One dives.

We almost always resurface, don't we? The loon
comes up near an island. Breathing again.

I want to speak to them. To know a love that means
three things at once and in entirety: dive, swim, breathe.

I paddle farther away from the dock. A loon's call
can't be replicated, only breathed in. I drift. The earth

is made of me, loons, and lake. This stillness
feels like lying in wait. Laughter from the dock is a call

for me to come back. And I want to. The loons realign,
almost touching, they drift: delicate, steady as a tended flame.

# V.

## Still Here Today

It takes fifty-three seconds to assemble an F-150. I was on a bridge
when one came at me and shattered my lower half.

I'm reminded of this because look at you now,
standing on remnants of a stone bridge over the Erie Canal.

A glare on the water is reflected light,
but it looks like the sun is split open and

leaking. Your arms are stretched wide and you're starting
at the beginning again, telling me about the creation

of the bridge. You speak of small miracles: stump-pullers
and oxen hauling earth with slip-scrapers. The cement was

waterproof! I'm smiling but rolling my eyes because that's how
these moments are built: you exclaim, I feign impatience.

How many F150s will drivers crash today? I should tell you
the truth. I love it here, on this two-hundred-year-old bridge.
I love oxen and limestone and the way you say *waterproof*.

## Last Night

The next day, we share a five-egg frittata on the front stoop.
Our young neighbor exclaims with joy, carrying a bird's nest

toward his sister, stick-thin arms outstretched.
All I know about eggs in nests is a robin's are blue.

The oak draws its shade over me. Inches away, the sun gets you—
I can feel it from here. Even today, you made me breakfast.

Last night, when you said *no*, I shouldn't have pressed
my body to yours to cry. It's just that I needed you to prove

my limbs to me. Even a breeze can dislodge a home
from its branch. You found our eggs at a farm stand

by the water—*Look!*—as you folded two dollars into the box—
*They're fresh!* A brook and a farm stand can be enough to deceive

those who seek peace, though naming it gives it walls and a roof.
I'm sorry about last night. The boy sings as he cradles

his tree-dead treasure. Please don't leave.

## Yoga for Poets

Twice today, I've encountered the etymology of the word
*Yoga*, which, I'm told, is born from the word *yolk*
and has to do with joining together. Breath and motion, oak
and earth. I read it first in an essay about poetry, then heard
it stated by a Barbie-bodied instructor in a pose she called lizard.
A coincidence, this fact finding me twice. I ended the workout soaked
in sweat and thinking about eggs. In my recent poetry, *yolk*
always means sunlight. A presence solitary and sure.

We yoke ourselves with meaning. For balance, like oxen along the Erie
Canal. One animal jolts and the buckets spill over. Look,
I know it's not a coincidence. Eggs keep appearing because I want a baby.
The guiding light in my poems no longer wants to be alone. I unhook
my neck, my hollow horns from the wooden U of the beam,
water splashing onto my feet, and the sun becomes a dewy chick, hatching.

# Stay

My father chooses rocks from the dirt and paints them. Each surface
must be timeworn and wide. Bottles of acrylic hues
crowd the other seat at his table: bottom lip bit, he mixes new blues.
When the rocks dry, he leaves them by streetlights or driveways,
the way his neighbors do. Calls it *planting*. Yesterday
he found one by his mailbox covered in the word Courage, and it grew
into the story he tells me now, in the creek, still wearing his shoes
but bellydeep and splashing. Daylight burns; the watertop radiates.

The injection sites on his stomach are bruised. I want to take flight.
When we get back, he'll pull me to the milkweed and start
talking about chrysalises, then forget the word *monarch*.
His worn-down hands crack open the plant's earlygreeen cone.
When I hand him the stone I chose at the creek, he says it looks like
a skull, but I tell him no. I want rock to stay rock, bone to stay bone.

## Mother

*i.*
At the dinner party, you served stew
on the good plates—
you have a cupboard of bowls,
but they're mismatched and chipped.

*ii.*
There's a photo of us reading in the bed
you pretended to share with him. My tiny
hands hold the book upside-down. You're
elsewhere entirely.

*iii.*
Things I love because of you:
irises, eating dinner outside,
coffee ice cream, being thanked,
special plates, glasses of wine.

*iv.*
All I could ever see of you
from the back seat was your right hand
on the wheel, tapping. I know how
your forehead wrinkles when you're singing.

*v.*
Things that make me think of you:
bathrobes, books with broken spines,
dried cranberries, my own eyes,
creaking floorboards, morning car rides.

*vi.*
You used to smoke cigarettes
in the dark after he yelled, and then
you'd chew cinnamon gum and sing
me to sleep with someone else's breath.

*vii.*
When you remarried, I wouldn't
pose for photos, and you made room
for my teenage angst to echo
off your first good love.

*viii.*
Things I hate because of you:
fake smiles, overstuffed pillows,
cold kitchens, glasses of wine,
getting ready, going the long way.

*ix.*
You and I could live in the sound
the evening ocean makes, the promise
in charcoal wind, cracked clam shells
made magical by moonlight.

*x.*
In the ocean, you are
the back of your head:
retreating, as the horizon
breathes you in.

## June 2020

When I'm warned that a movie includes graphic content,
my body believes I'm about to be hit by a truck again.

On the screen, a yellowed room must be lit by headlights
headed toward me. A close-up of the wife

chopping garlic turns into metal parts splitting skin.
Outside the shot, everyone's bleeding.

But it's just a murder scene.
I don't know how to see graphic content

without remembering the night you saved my life.
I don't know how to protest all cops besides you.

When you asked if your wife could read my essay aloud
at a rally to support the State Troops,

I didn't want her to. The night of the crash, I told you
I couldn't breathe, and you said *yes you can*. In the essay,

I thank you. But now, when I see the words I Can't Breathe
printed on someone's shirt, or hear them chanted on the news,

I think about who's been shot before I think about you.

## Set This to Music and Sing to It

I want to pull over and write a poem about you.
Someone once told me that braking on the highway means you're doing something wrong.
When I told my dentist I write poetry, he told me I should write songs.
Set this one to something good and turn it up.
I've never liked knowing I'm doing something wrong.
Before I left, you told me I'm your rock.
Before I left, you ran your finger along the curve of my nose.
In the dentist's office, they were playing bad rock.
If I try to write about you, it'll be wrong.
I don't know if that would change if this were a song.
My dad told me he used to have a pet rock—
if we tell someone that something is worth loving, that can sometimes be enough.
I'm sorry the dentist showed up in this poem.
If we tell a poet to write a song, what could've been music turns into mechanics.
And what kind of job is a dentist doing, anyway?
Spending all day talking to people who can't answer back.
I'm not going to pull over, I'm just going to head back.

## My New Supermarket, Vergennes VT

The wheels on all the carts stick.
Or maybe I get the same cart every time.

Outside, mountains bloom from treetops
and flocks of birds mark the line

where dusk begins in the sky. A woman
nudges by me, three pumpkins in her basket

and now she's buying frosting. I imagine her house,
built by Bob down the road, wood-shingled, blue trim

on the windows and every spider web has been swept out.
My friend once found a spider dead in my shower,

considered it a bad omen and ate it. If I ate a whole pumpkin,
maybe I'd look pregnant and have a house. More likely,

I'd end up a jack-o-lantern: fire-eyed and smiling
on the stoop of someone else's glowing home.

The fluorescent lights here make 2% milk tricky to find.
Everything's misplaced: coffee used to be one aisle over

from Baking Needs. Seltzer should be at the end.

Above, the ceiling says it's happy to have us,
and thanks us for shopping. I say, *Frankly, I dreaded this,*

and it says, *Go back.* It's not until a flanneled teen reaches
over me, that I realize I've been feeling up plums

for five minutes. I unstick my cart and head toward
the tortillas, pretending to know what I'm making.

## We Call It Beautiful

Today, the sunflower
echoes the aging banana on our counter,

each one speckling into death.
I think of death

differently every day. My father's
voice on the phone as he lies flat

on the hardwood floor,
straightening out his collapsing spine.

My mother's wet eyes staring into the empty
mouth of her wine glass.

My grandmother is the ceiling
I lift my eyes to.

How it will happen to me,
or how it cannot happen to you.

## Everything Alive

The kitten's sick. Turns out the plants are toxic. No one gave me the master list of things that poison kittens. But now I know the truth about chives, dental floss, tinsel, and tulips.

She did nothing to deserve this. The plants did nothing to deserve exile, but now they're out on the deck—they'll freeze to death.

And the kitten is pawing at the floor around her food. It's a burial instinct—a wild cat digs a half-eaten pigeon into the dirt so no one else gets it. I read that floor-pawing is "obsolete in captivity."

In our home, the kitten paws the wood floor as if she might push something aside and find safety. But her predators are locked on the porch. Houseplants held hostage out in the wild.

When Pete and Kate had their baby, their cat started pissing all over the floor. They tried separating baby and cat, but that didn't stop it, so they gave the cat back.

I'll build a house for my plants out on the deck. I'll keep the tinsel and floss in the freezer. The plants will warm up, the kitten will live, I'll give birth to my son, and I'll never stop holding him.

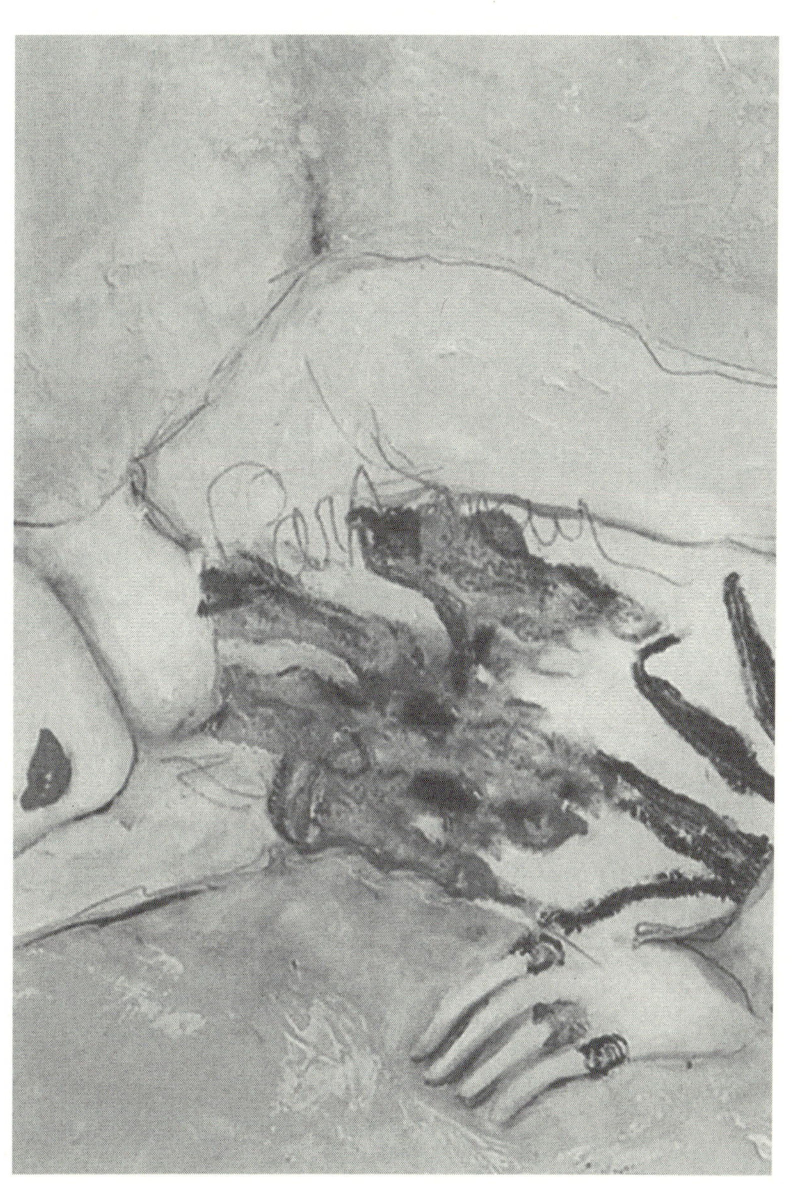

# Acknowledgments

Thank you to the editors of the following journals, workshops, newsletters, and programs for supporting the work in this collection: Bixby Writers, Bread Loaf School of English, *Cider Press Review, Identity Theory, Indiana Review,* Kenyon Review Writers Workshop, *Mortar Magazine*, St. Lawrence Press, *Sycamore Review,* The Small Bow, and *Zig Zag Lit Mag.*

The Green Writers Press team showed this book love when I didn't have any left for it. Thank you, Maria Tane, for your careful, encouraging edits, and Haley Hutchinson for your enthusiastic and skilled support with publicity. Deanna Perlov, you're going places. GWP founder and cover designer Dede Cummings, you are force of nature. "Thank you" barely touches the surface.

No art could be more fitting for this book's cover than Leigh Veiner's gorgeous work.

I am indebted to the teachers from high school through higher education: Catherine Reed, Annie Funnell, Paul Hendrickson,

Tracy K. Smith, Jenny Offill, Sigrid Nunez, Brooks Haxton, Bruce Smith, and Mary Karr. My own students, past and present, continue to inspire me.

Utmost gratitude to Christopher Kennedy. Thank you for deep attention, respect, and care over many years, and for your words about this collection.

Natalie Shapero, you said I had a book in me one way or another, and I decided to believe you. Here it is. Thank you.

My cohort at Syracuse University: Jacob Gedetsis, Sara Potocsny, and Ejiofor Ugwu, thank you for reading and improving so much of what's in these pages. Fellow Syracuse poets Eve Payne and Bridget O'Bernstein, I am in awe of you and your work. Grady Chambers, from a first phone call about Syracuse to a book blurb—your kindness is steady and generous.

Sydney Rende, thank you for motivating me to fight for my book and for having dinner with me almost every night for over two years. Jackson Frons, you have a big heart you don't want us to know about, but I'm grateful for it.

To Terry Bilsky, Steve Carmichael, Clarkson Collins, Sara Chimene-Weiss, Anita Doar, Tom Dreisbach, Jude Dry, Natasha Gallipeau, Maura Goldstein, Becca Greenfield, Danny Hurwitz, Hannah Johnsen, Hannah Longman, Elise Morocco, Alexander Manshel, "Matt is Typing," Lisa Newby, Kelly Stout, Maggie Tishman, Lucy Voorhees, and Caire Webb, for cheering for me throughout the decade it took to bring this book to life.

Thanks to Zach Williams for early reads of my work and a deep, exasperating friendship. And to my dear friend Margaret Ray, my gratitude is fierce. You are at the heart of my poetry world.

To the Conlin family, Julia Fisher, James Jorgensen, Michael Leslie, Aaron Matthew, Leslie Ricky, Mike Walsh, all the first responders, and the entire Yale New Haven Hospital care team: you saved my life. Thank you.

Homer, I'm grateful we're in this together.

Mom and Dad, you showed me why to love writing. You showed me how and why to love.

Emma Carmichael. Look at us. I'm seer.

Lee, Morgan, and Misha, my boundless love.

# About the Author

MOLLY JOHNSEN is a Vermont-based writer and teacher. Her work has appeared in the *Nashville Review, Indiana Review, Cider Press Review,* and others. A previous version of *Everything Alive* was selected as a semi-finalist for the Black Lawrence Press St. Lawrence Book Award. She holds an MFA from Syracuse University.